Where We Work

by Joy Darlington

Editorial Offices: Glenview, Illinois • Parsippany, New Jersey • New York, New York
Sales Offices: Needham, Massachusetts • Duluth, Georgia • Glenview, Illinois
Coppell, Texas • Ontario, California • Mesa, Arizona

Come and learn about our many different **jobs**! See where we work. See what we do.

Meet Joe. He works in a busy factory. He makes crayons in many different colors. You can use these crayons to color!

Here is Emma at the daycare center in her home. She takes care of small children while their parents work. Emma keeps the children safe and happy.

Meet Maria. She is a plumber. She uses **tools**, like her wrench, to fix leaks. She can fix broken pipes too!

Here is Oliver. Oliver is a **volunteer** at a hospital. He works for free. He helps patients by reading to them. He talks to them and makes them smile.

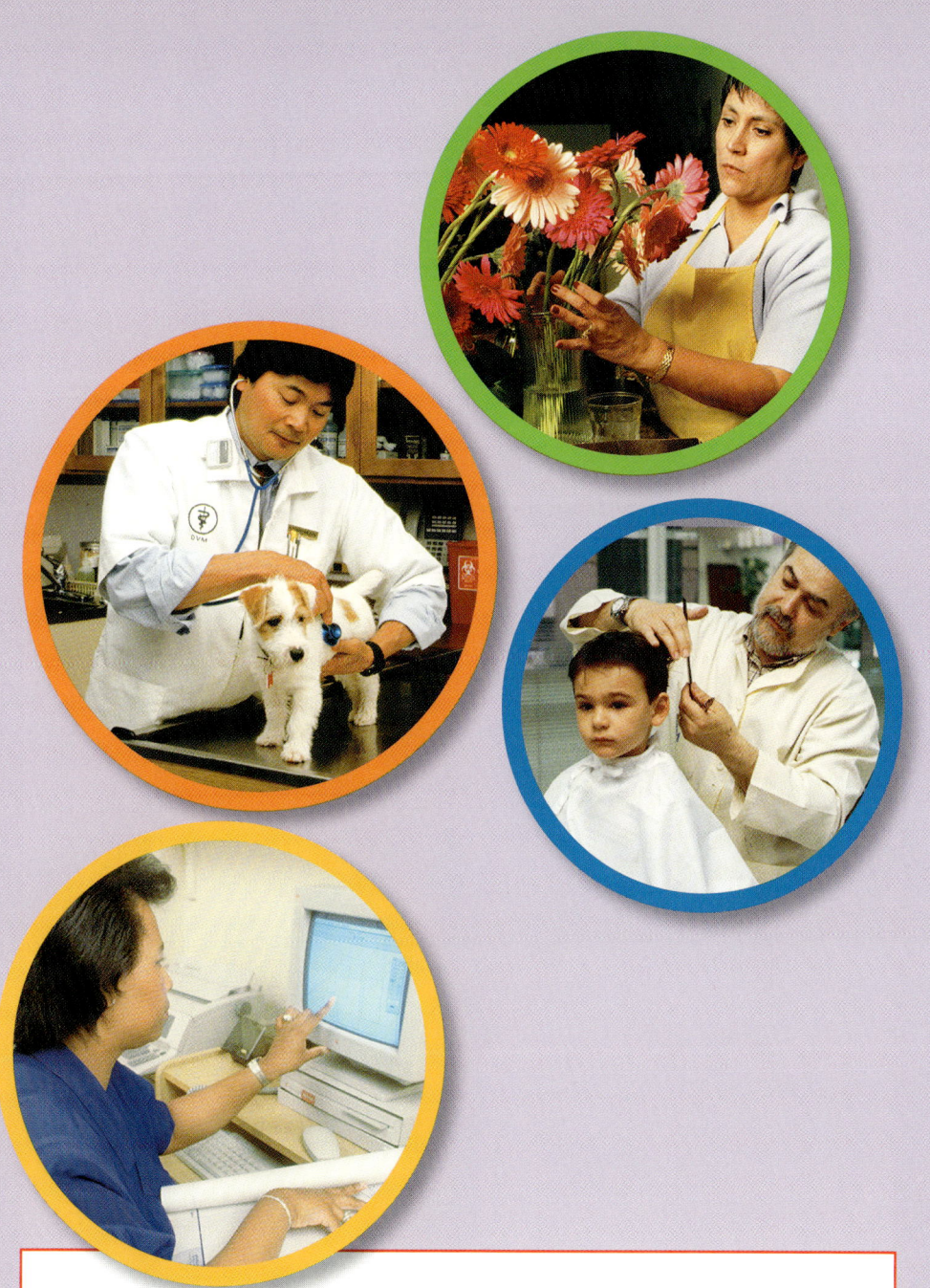

What job do you think you would like to do when you are a grownup? Why?

Glossary

jobs the work people do

tools things that are used to help people do work

volunteer a person who works for free

Where We Work

by Joy Darlington

Editorial Offices: Glenview, Illinois • Parsippany, New Jersey • New York, New York
Sales Offices: Needham, Massachusetts • Duluth, Georgia • Glenview, Illinois
Coppell, Texas • Ontario, California • Mesa, Arizona

Where We Work

by Joy Darlington

PEARSON
Scott Foresman

Editorial Offices: Glenview, Illinois • Parsippany, New Jersey • New York, New York
Sales Offices: Needham, Massachusetts • Duluth, Georgia • Glenview, Illinois
Coppell, Texas • Ontario, California • Mesa, Arizona